5.99.

# The Native Peoples of North America

**MARTYN WHITTOCK**

Hodder & Stoughton

A MEMBER OF THE HODDER HEADLINE GROUP

# Acknowledgements

For Donna, Jim, Corinne and Carolyn; with fond memories of the warmth of Californian friendship and Californian sunshine!
The author would like to thank Frank E Weingart at Coloma State Park (Sutter's Mill) California, for so kindly taking an interest in enquiries and following up the request for information regarding John Sutter. Also thanks to the staff at Sutter's Fort, Sacramento, for providing such a vivid insight into California of the 1840s and to the staff at the American Museum in Britain, Claverton, Bath, for help and flexibility in the effort to make Native American topics as accessible as possible to students.

The publishers would like to thank the following individuals, institutions and companies for permission to reproduce copyright illustrations in this book:
The front cover shows Tochtaw Indians in 'Indian Ball Games' by George Catlin, reproduced courtesy of The Art Archive, and inset an engraving by Karl Bodmer of 'Wakusasse' a Musquake Indian, reproduced courtesy of The Bridgeman Art Library.

Actionplus Sports Images, page 3 (bottom right); American Indian Review, 'Dancing For My Relatives' by Jim Yellowhawk, page 2 and 'The World is in Your Hands' by Sean Couchie, page 45 (top left); Associated Press Perfect Image, page 7 (top); The Bridgeman Art Library/Private Collection, 'Commanche Village' by George Catlin, page 11; The Bridgeman Art Library/Private Collection, 'Blackfoot Medicine Man' by George Catlin, page 15; The Bridgeman Art Library/Private Collection, 'Custer's Last Stand' by Edgar Paxon, page 38; The British Museum, page 12; Burton Historical Collection, Detroit Public Library, page 36 (top); Corbis, page 44 (left and right); Walt Disney Co, pages 26 and 27; Fotomas Index, page 5 (bottom); Historical Picture Archive/CORBIS, page 3 (bottom); Hulton Archive, pages 10, 13, 35, 36, 43 (top); Klamath County Museum, Oregon, page 43 (bottom left); McFarlin Library, University of Tulsa, page 42 (bottom right); Maxwell Museum of Anthropology, University of New Mexico, page 7 (bottom); Musee de l'Homme, page 17; National Anthropological Archives, Smithsonian Institution, page 40, MS 2367 – A, No. 08570400 (bottom left); National Geographic, page 40 (bottom right); Nebraska State Historical Society, page 43 (top right); Peter Newark's American Pictures, pages 20 (right), 30, 40 (top), 41 (top right); Frederic Remington/Peter Newark's American Pictures, page 42 (top right); The Stapleton Collection/The Bridgeman Art Library, 'Bison-Dance of the Mandan Indians' by Karl Bodmer, page 14, 'Mato-Tope, Adorned with the Insignia of his Warlike Deeds' by Karl Bodmer, page 19, 'Pehriska-Rupha, Miniture Warrior in the Costume of the Dog Dance' by Karl Bodmer, page 20 (left); Twentieth Century Fox/Roland Grant Archive, page 3 (top right); University of Michigan Museum of Art/The Bridgeman Art Library, 'The Attack on the Emigrant Train' by Charles Ferdinand Wilmar, page 34; University of Pennsylvania Museum, page 43 (bottom left); Werner Forman Archive, page16; Western History Collections, University of Oklahoma Libraries, page 37; West Point Military Academy USA/Bridgeman Art Library, 'Scalping' by P Rindisbacher, page 18; West Point Museum Art Collection, United States Military Academy, page 39.

The publishers would also like to thank the following for permission to reproduce material in this book:
Alfred A Knopf Inc/Random House for extracts from Lewis and ClarkLewis and Clark by D Duncans and K Burns – Alfred A Knopf, 1997; Dorling Kindersley for extracts from Native American Indians by D Murdoch – ©1995 Dorling Kindersley Ltd, London; National Geographic Society for the extracts from National Geographic Vol.170, No.6, December 1986; Pearson Education for extracts from History of the USA by H Brogan – Longman, 1985.

Please note that some sources have been adapted to make them more accessible to students.

Every effort has been made to trace and acknowledge ownership of copyright. The publishers will be glad to make suitable arrangements with any copyright holders whom it has not been able to contact.

Orders: please contact Bookpoint Ltd, 130 Milton Park, Abingdon, Oxon OX14 4SB.
Telephone: (44) 01235 827720, Fax: (44) 01235 400454. Lines are open from 9.00 – 6.00, Monday to Saturday, with a 24 hour message answering service.
Email address: orders@bookpoint.co.uk

*British Library Cataloguing in Publication Data*
A catalogue record for this title is available from The British Library

ISBN 0 340 80330 4

First published 2002

| Impression number | 10 9 8 7 6 5 4 3 2 1 |
| Year | 2008 2007 2006 2005 2004 2003 2002 |

Typeset by Liz Rowe.
Printed in Great Britain for Hodder & Stoughton Educational, a division of Hodder Headline Plc, 338 Euston Road, London NW1 3BH by Printer Trento.

# Contents

## THIS CHAPTER ASKS
What images do we have of Native Americans?

### NEW WORDS

**HOLLYWOOD:** the area of the USA famous for its film studios.
**IMAGES:** a mental picture, or set of ideas.
**REDSKINS:** White nickname for Native Americans – offensive to them as it comes from a time when Whites were rewarded for the number of 'Indians' they could kill and skin.
**'WALK OF FAME':** the part of Hollywood Boulevard, Los Angeles, where film stars' names are recorded in metal stars on the pavement.

### WHAT'S IN YOUR MIND?

Long before the first Europeans travelled to America, Native Americans lived there. These are the people whom we often refer to as 'Indians'. Even if you have never studied Native Americans before, you will probably have **images** of 'Indians' in your mind.

Before you begin to find out more about Native Americans, it is a good idea to think about the different kinds of images that books, films or TV present of them. Then think about what images you have in your mind already. After you have found out more about Native American 'Indians', you may decide that some of these images are correct. You may decide that some of them are wrong and misleading.

### SOURCE A

**AMERICAN INDIAN REVIEW**
SUMMER 1999                                    No. 21

| UK | £3.50 |
| USA | $5.00 |
| Canada | $6.50 |
| France | fr 30.00 |
| Germany | mk 8.50 |
| Iceland | kr 450 |
| Ireland | pt 4.20 |
| Italy | lira 9580 |
| Japan | yen 720 |
| Netherlands | fl 10 |
| South Africa | rd 27 |
| Switzerland | fr 7.50 |

0  07447 08346

Although films about 'Indians' have been made since the earliest days of **Hollywood**, it wasn't until 1979 that a Native American actor, named Jay Silverheels, got his name included on the metal stars in Hollywood's **'Walk of Fame'**. Jay played Tonto in *The Lone Ranger*, a popular 1950s TV programme.

◄ *Cover of* American Indian Review *(1999) showing* 'Dancing for my Relatives' *by Jim Yellowhawk.*

## SOURCE B

▲ *Native American Barbie Doll, 2001.*

## SOURCE C

◄ *Badge of the US football team the Washington Redskins, shown on a player's helmet.*

## SOURCE D

◄ *Native American warriors from the film 'Last of the Mohicans'.*

## SOURCE E

▲ *'The Buffalo Hunter', by Seth Eastman.*

**Q**

**1.** Make a spidergram showing all the things you associate with Native American 'Indians'. Then explain where you have got these ideas from.

**2.** Look at **Sources A–E**. If you were a modern Native American which of these 'images' would you approve of, which would you disapprove of?

Explain why.

# What's in a name?

We often call the people living in the Americas when the first Europeans arrived by the name 'Indians'. But, of course, they do not live in India. Something very odd is going on here. We need to ask:

- How did they ever get called by this name?
- Does it matter?
- If it matters what name should we use instead of this one?

## A PROBLEM READING THE MAP

The first modern European to discover America was Christopher Columbus, in 1492. He was an explorer looking for a quicker way to reach eastern Asia (the East Indies). He hoped that if he could do this he would be able to more easily bring back Asian spices and gold to Europe. Columbus persuaded King Ferdinand and Queen Isabella of Spain to pay for his expedition.

Columbus believed that if he sailed westward from Spain he would eventually reach China. There was only one problem with this idea – the continent of America was in the way. Of course, Columbus did not know this. As a result, when he landed on the Caribbean island of Hispaniola, on 12 October, 1492, he thought he was somewhere near China! As a result the people that he met he called 'Indians' because he thought they lived in the East Indies. The name stuck. In 1499 and 1501 another explorer, Amerigo Vespucci, carried out a similar journey. In time he gave his name to America. So, 'America' is a Spanish name and the people living there were named after India. All a bit of a muddle.

What was not muddled was Columbus' determination to steal gold from the people of Hispaniola. He cut off the hands of those aged over 14 who failed to bring in enough gold and hunted any who tried to escape with dogs. By 1494, 500,000 people (half the island's population) had been killed by the Spanish, or had committed **suicide**.

## DOES A NAME MATTER?

To many 'Indians' it matters a lot. They do not see Columbus' arrival as anything to celebrate and don't want to be named after his map-reading problems! More importantly they had and have their own names for themselves.

19th-century Americans called the Salish native people the 'Flatheads' because of a mistake translating languages. The Salish do not have flat heads at all!

## NEW WORDS

**LOINCLOTH:** a small piece of cloth to cover a person's private parts.
**SUICIDE:** to kill yourself.

## SOURCE A

On the 34th day we sighted land. And there I found very many islands filled with countless people. And I have taken possession of all of them for their Highnesses [Ferdinand and Isabella] with the royal flag unfurled and with no opposition.

▲ *Written by Columbus in 1492.*

## SOURCE B

We're even called Indians because some poor guy got lost and the first people he bumped into he called 'Indians'. At least, he thought they were, and the name has stuck.

▲ *Robbie Niquanicappo, a Cree Native American.*

## SOURCE C

O most excellent gold! Whoever has gold has a treasure which gives him the power to get what he wants. It lets him do what he wants in the world and even helps souls into heaven.

▲ *Written by Columbus.*

## COMPLICATIONS, COMPLICATIONS

The peoples of the Americas never had one name to describe themselves. Instead, different tribes had names for themselves. Many of these names, in their own languages, meant something like, 'the people', 'our people', 'the real human beings'. Others took their names from their character (like bravery), where they lived, what kinds of lives they lived (such as hunters, or farmers).

Even using Native American names can be a problem. Some of the names picked up by Europeans were not what a tribe of Native Americans called themselves but what they were called by their Native American neighbours, or enemies. So, the Native Americans called the 'Sioux', actually called themselves the Lakota, Dakota and Nakota. 'Sioux' was a name given them by their Ojibwa enemies. It means 'enemy', or 'snake'! To make things more complicated, tribes were often made up of many smaller bands (groups). In this way, the tribe of the Lakota was made up of seven smaller bands, such as the Oglala, and Hunkpapa.

Other complications come from names being changed as they passed into the Spanish, English or French languages. Sometimes today a name is used because a group of Native Americans speak the same language. The problem is that although they may speak a similar language, it does not mean they are part of the same tribe, so the name may not be an accurate one to use for them.

### WHAT NAME SHOULD WE USE?

There is no agreement as to what name should be used. Some people think we are just stuck with the word 'Indians'. Others argue that 'Native Americans' is better, or 'First Americans', or 'Native American Indians'. There is no definite answer. In this book we will use the name 'Native Americans', to describe people generally, but wherever possible will use the name of the tribe, or band.

**Q**

**1.** Explain why Columbus used the name 'Indians'.

**2.** What impressions do **Sources A** and **C** give of Columbus' motives?

**3.** How useful is **Source D** to a modern historian?

**4.** Explain why many modern Native Americans object to the name 'Indian'.

**a.** Mention how it arose.

**b.** Describe how it links to bad treatment.

**c.** Explain what native names were really used.

**d.** Decide a better name than 'Indians'.

**SOURCE D**

▲ *A picture of Arawak tribespeople greeting Columbus after he landed on the island of Hispaniola, in 1492. They are shown giving him gold and jewels. In fact the picture was drawn by a Belgian in 1594. The Arawaks actually gave Columbus parrots, spears and cloth. And they were not wearing loincloths but feathers and body paint.*

# The first Americans

**YOUR MISSION: to look at all the evidence and decide who were the first people to reach America.**

## NEW WORDS

**MONGOLIAN:** people from central Asia.

When Columbus reached America he met Native Americans who had already been there for thousands of years. But when did the first people reach America? Where did they come from? There is a lot of debate about both these questions.

For a long time scientists and archaeologists thought the matter was fairly simple. People first travelled to America from Asia in about 18,000BC. They were Asian people who crossed to America when the Ice Age caused the sea level to drop. Due to this there was a 'land bridge' that connected Asia and America.

At the end of the Ice Age this 'land bridge' was flooded and contact was broken until a few Vikings settled briefly in Newfoundland around AD1000 and later, Columbus arrived in AD1492. Recent research has made the matter more complicated, as you will see.

## SOURCE A

People probably reached North America about 20,000 years ago, by means of a land bridge that existed then between Siberia and Alaska (the plain of Beringia, where the Bering Straits are now) and a corridor between the ice sheets of Canada and Alaska.

▲ **The Newnes Historical Atlas,** *1983.*

## SOURCE B

So much water had gone into the making of the great northern ice-cap that the oceans receded from the shallow Bering Straights, and early **Mongolians**, it is thought, moved across the land bridge. The Bering crossing may have begun before 40,000BC.

▲ *H.Brogan,* **History of the USA,** *1985.*

## SOURCE C

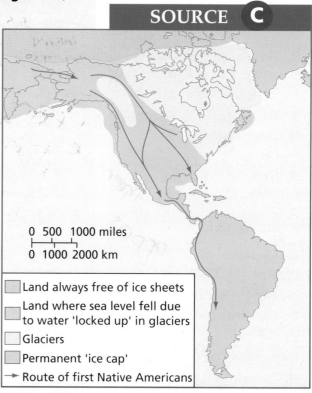

0 500 1000 miles
0 1000 2000 km

☐ Land always free of ice sheets
☐ Land where sea level fell due to water 'locked up' in glaciers
☐ Glaciers
☐ Permanent 'ice cap'
→ Route of first Native Americans

▲ *Map showing the traditional idea of how the first people reached America.*

## SOURCE D

The genetic findings were announced earlier this year by Theodore Schuur from the Emory University in Atlanta, USA. If the findings hold up, populations from Europe and the Middle East now seem to have been among the North American continent's early settlers.

▲ Athena Review, *1999. Schuur studied bones found near Kennewick, Washington, dating from about 7,300BC.*

## SOURCE E

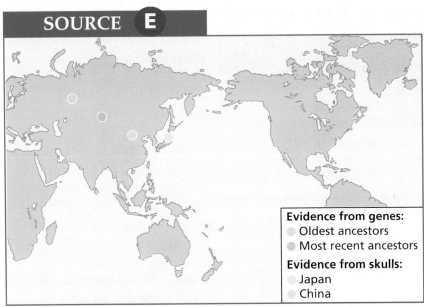

Evidence from genes:
- Oldest ancestors
- Most recent ancestors

Evidence from skulls:
- Japan
- China

⋏ *Places where Native Americans may have originated, using work by The American Society of Human Genetics,1999 and University of Michigan, 2000.*

## SOURCE G

The first humans to enter America have no obvious links to any Asian groups. This could be because they have been separated from where they came from in Asia for the longest period of time.

⋏ *Research by the University of Michigan on ancient and modern skulls, 2000.*

## SOURCE H

⋏ *The earliest weapons. The top one from Folsom, New Mexico, dates from about 8000BC. The lower one is from Clovis, New Mexico and dates from about 10,000BC.*

## SOURCE F

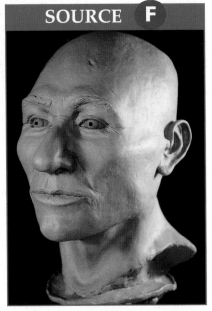

⋏ *Artist's reconstruction of the face of a skull, found by the Columbia River, Washington, in 1996. Called 'Kennewick Man', the bones have caused a huge row. Some scientists think he was European not Asian. Native Americans want to rebury the bones, while some scientists want to study them. US law allows such bones to be reburied by Native Americans. The bones date from about 7,300BC – the oldest bones found in America.*

## ℐNVESTIGATION

**You are the investigator!**

You are an archaeologist trying to make sense of the evidence and the problems.

- What is the oldest evidence for human bones and weapons in North America?
- What is the traditional way of explaining where these first Americans came from?
- What parts of this idea have been challenged? Why have they been challenged?
- What different parts of the world might the first Americans have come from?
- What difficulties face you in studying these ancient bones of Native Americans?

## THIS CHAPTER ASKS

How did different environments affect Native American lifestyles and beliefs?

What evidence is there for the movement of Native American people before the expansion of European settlements?

What part did warfare play in the lives of Native Americans?

## MANY 'WORLDS'... MANY PEOPLES ...

North America is huge. It is as far from modern New York to San Francisco, as it is from London to New York. It is made up of many different landscapes and climates. In the north is the frozen arctic; in the South-West is desert; swamps cover great areas of the South-East; while vast forests spread across the Pacific North-West; and, on the Plains are natural grasslands.

Modern California is so fertile and warm that every fruit (except bananas) will grow there. It has always been a popular place to live. More Native Americans lived in what is now California than in the rest of what is now the USA put together!

A

B

C

D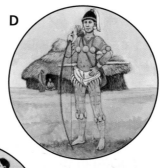

E

F

G

H

I

J

These different environments supported many different Native American lifestyles. There was never one way of life for Native Americans. These different groups of people lived in what we call 'tribes' and these were often made up of smaller bands. Some were large; others very small. There were over 600 of these 'tribes'. Together, they spoke over 500 different languages. Some were farmers; others hunters. Some were settled; others were always on the move. Some were peaceful; others were warlike. All had a close relationship with nature and the world in which they lived.

**Q**

**1.** Choose three of the different environment areas. For each one:

■ Describe what it was like (e.g. hot/cold, plants growing there).

■ Explain how each environment led to a different Native American lifestyle (e.g. kinds of houses, ways of life).

**2.** From the information in this BIG PICTURE, explain why we cannot treat Native Americans as if they were all 'the same'.

**Discussion Point**
Why is it that the lives of modern British people <u>seem</u> less affected by their environment than people in the past?

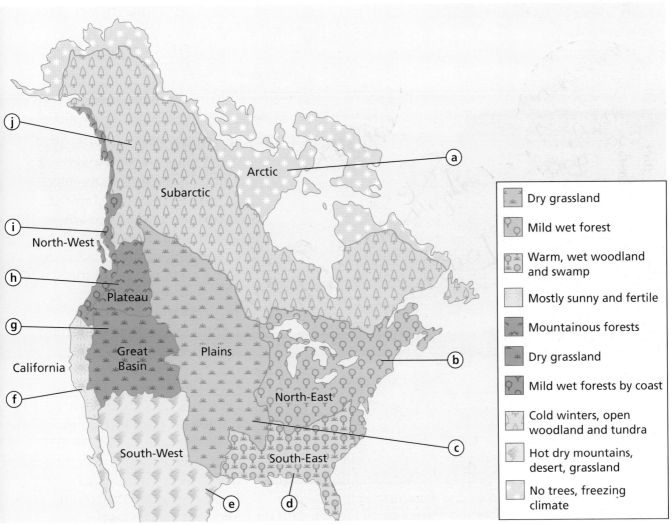

**Legend:**
- Dry grassland
- Mild wet forest
- Warm, wet woodland and swamp
- Mostly sunny and fertile
- Mountainous forests
- Dry grassland
- Mild wet forests by coast
- Cold winters, open woodland and tundra
- Hot dry mountains, desert, grassland
- No trees, freezing climate

▲ *Different environment areas of North America. Page 8 shows modern pictures of some of the 600 tribes and the different lifestyles supported by these different areas.*

# Different lifestyles

## DIFFERENT LANDS, DIFFERENT LIVES

Where do you live? Would you live the same kind of life if you lived on top of a mountain? Or in a jungle clearing? Or on a remote island? Think about it. The chances are that if you lived in one of these places you might have to change one, or two, things about your life in order to survive!

Different groups of Native Americans, in different parts of North America, lived very different lives. This is because their lives were shaped by the **environment** in which they lived. This affected how they organised their lives, the food they ate, the clothes they wore, the places in which they lived. We are going to look at three very different groups of Native American peoples as they were when Europeans first met them. They lived in very different environments:

1. the Plains
2. the North-East Woodlands
3. the South-West deserts and mountains.

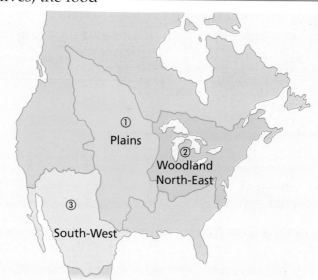

① Plains
② Woodland North-East
③ South-West

## SOURCE A

▲ *Mandan village, painted by the American artist, George Catlin, in the 1830s. The painting shows earth lodges, buffalo skulls, sacred poles, a burial ground with bodies left to rot in the open air.*

## 1. LIVING ON THE PLAINS

The Plains are a great area of rolling grassland in the heart of North America. Many of the tribes living there when the first Europeans met them in the 19th century had once lived on the edges of the Plains in settled villages, mixing farming with hunting. The most important animal hunted was the buffalo, which roamed the Plains in their millions. For centuries these had been hunted on foot. In fact, much of the grassland was created by Native Americans setting fire to the vegetation to encourage animals to come and feed on the tender new grass – and be killed by hunters!

**10**

SOURCE **B**

▲ *Comanche village of 'tipi' tents, with buffalo hides being cleaned and dried. Painted by George Catlin in the 1830s.*

## FROM FOOT TO HORSE

From about 1720 this changed. Horses lost by early Spanish settlers began to be used by some Native Americans, which transformed their lives. Tribes such as the Arapaho, Blackfeet, Cheyenne, Comanche, Crow and Lakota (called 'Sioux' by their enemies) gave up farming and became **nomadic** hunters, following the buffalo and living in 'tipis' made from buffalo hide. In fact the buffalo supplied almost all their needs. Its fur and hide provided clothes, blankets, shelter; its meat gave food; bones gave tools and arrow heads; hooves were used as tools and rattles, or boiled to make glue; tails made fly swats; dung was burned as fuel.

The population of Plains Native Americans went up as more moved onto the Plains. Between 1800 and 1850 about 50% of the buffalo on the Plains were killed by these Plains tribes. Some tribes though, such as the Mandan, Pawnee and Hidatsa, continued the old way of life. They lived in permanent villages growing crops such as maize, and hunting for only part of the year.

In the 1970s the US government had to return to the Native American tradition of setting fire to the grass of the Plains. Without this the grassland in many places was turning into woodland!

**Q** **1.** Look at **Sources A** and **B**. Explain how the different ways the Mandan and Comanche used their environment created different kinds of villages.

**2.** Why was the horse so important to Plains tribes?

**3.** A modern historian described the buffalo as 'a walking department store'. Explain how this was true for tribes on the Plains.

**11**

THINKING IT THROUGH

## 2. LIVING IN THE WOODS

The environment of the North-East Woodland tribes such as the Mohawk, Huron, Iroquois, Micmac, Pequot and Powhatan was very different to that of the tribes living on the Plains. For these people wood was a valuable resource. Trees provided wood for bows, arrows, **toboggans**, the framework of **wigwams** and longhouses (covered with bark) where many people could live together. Bark was also used to make superb canoes that were tough but very lightweight. Villages were often surrounded by wooden fences for defence.

### HUNTERS AND FARMERS

The woods also provided animals to hunt. For centuries Native Americans had burnt the forest to clear away brambles and bushes. This made it easier for deer to feed – and be hunted. Otter and bear were also hunted for their fur. Fish were caught in lakes and rivers.

Most Woodland tribes also used 'slash and burn' agriculture – clearing the ground with fire. They grew maize, beans and pumpkins.

### POWERFUL WOMEN

Amongst the Iroquois the farming was organised by the women. The Iroquois were a combination of five tribes (Mohawk, Onondaga, Seneca, Oneida, Cayuga) who had come together to end the warfare that had plagued their lives. The legendary Mohawk, Hiawatha, had organised the **alliance**. Each tribe ruled itself but important decisions were made by a Great Council. Its members were men but they were chosen (and if necessary removed) by the elder women of the tribe.

### NEW WORDS

**ALLIANCE:** a friendship agreement.
**TOBOGGAN:** a sledge for crossing snow.
**WIGWAM:** round framework of poles covered by reed mats or bark.

### SOURCE C

One of the reasons they did that burning was to make it easier to hunt the animals that were part of their lives. There was a deliberate act by native peoples to create a particular type of forest to help their lives.

▲ *William Cronon in* Natural Born Americans, *Channel 4, 2000, describes burning the forest.*

### SOURCE D

▲ *English drawing of Algonkian (a Woodland people) longhouses, 1585.*

### SOURCE E

▲ *English drawing of fishing using spears, and a 'fish trap', 1585.*

## 3. LIVING IN THE DESERT

The Native Americans of the South-West lived in a land of mountains and desert. It was a land of blazing sunshine in summer and cold in winter. Those living there when the first Europeans (the Spanish) arrived were an ancient farming people. Their ancestors had built impressive towns of finely cut stone, such as that at Chaco Canyon and Mesa Verde. In fact the Spanish name for these people was 'Pueblo' meaning 'town'. Many of those living there continued to build towns and farm the land growing maize, melons, beans, pumpkins and cotton. They watered their fields using channels that carried the precious water to their crops. Their houses had no doors and the upper floors were reached by ladders.

Tribes such as the Yuman and Quechan (called Mohave by outsiders) lived in simpler earth-covered houses, and mixed farming with gathering wild berries.

## HUNTERS AND RAIDERS

From about AD1400 these farmers were raided by fierce warriors moving south. These were the Apache and Navajo. They lived in simple huts, or 'wickiups', made from brushwood, and hunted and collected wild plants. Some, such as the Apache bands of the Mescalero and Lipan lived in buffalo-hide tipis, like Plains tribes.

The Apache had travelled far to reach the South-West. Other speakers of their group of languages lived in Canada, on the edge of the Arctic!

**SOURCE** **F**

▲ *Mesa Verde cliff town, abandoned by* AD*1300.*

**Q**

**1.** Explain how and why the Native Americans of:

**a.** the Woodland North-East, and

**b.** the South-West

had very different lives compared with those of the Plains tribes.

**2.** From the evidence, explain how Native Americans changed, as well as were affected by, their environment. Think about: the use of fire, the use of water, buildings, effects on animals.

**Discussion Point**
What modern invention do you think most influences your lifestyle? Why?

# How did environment affect beliefs?

## A WORLD OF SPIRIT BEINGS

When the Walt Disney filmmakers wanted to show Native American beliefs, they made their cartoon heroine, Pocahontas, sing: 'I know every rock and tree and creature has a life, has a spirit, has a name'.

Native Americans believed that gods, spirits and **supernatural** heroes were all around them. They believed that different spirit beings brought good things, such as food, and bad things, such as diseases. Because of this, Native Americans spent a great deal of time trying to live and act in a way they believed would influence these spirits to help them. These special ways of acting (special words, songs, clothing, dances, objects) we call **ritual**.

There was never one religion that united all Native Americans. But most had a belief in a supreme **creator** and then many other spirits, which inhabited animals and other natural objects. There were, though, many different beliefs amongst different tribes. Many of these were beliefs aimed at explaining the 'world' in which they lived. It was another way by which different environments shaped their lives and understanding of the world.

## 1. SPIRIT OF THE BUFFALO

The lives of the tribes on the Plains were dominated by the buffalo. And so were their beliefs. Tribes such as the Lakota, Cheyenne and Mandan believed that their hunts would only be successful if they were carried out 'respectfully'. This meant carrying out ritual dances and songs before the hunt. If they did so, they believed, the buffalo would give up their lives to the hunters.

### NEW WORDS

**CREATOR:** maker of the world.
**MEDICINE:** power given by a spirit being.
**RITUAL:** something done in a very special way designed to show what you believe.
**SUPERNATURAL:** a spirit being.

In some tribes young men would give their wives to old men for the night. They believed the old man's hunting skill would pass into the woman and then into the young man.

### SOURCE A

▲ *Buffalo Bull Dance of the Mandan. Painted by Karl Bodmer, 1833.*

## DANCES AND VISIONS

Most Plains tribes believed that the great dome of the sky was the home of the Creator, who was called 'Wakan' by the Lakota. Below this were star gods, and below this spirits. Medicine men, or shamans, believed they had the power to communicate with these spirits and could cure illness. From mountain tribes, such as the Shoshone and Salish came the belief in Coyote, the trickster, and his adventures.

It was also thought that before a boy could become a man he must have a vision. Going alone into the wild country, without food, he would wait until some unusual experience seemed to show an animal spirit communicating to him. This then became his special **medicine**. A sign or symbol of that animal would then be carried in a special medicine bag. This was thought to give protection and good luck. Men who had seen the same vision, or dream, would form Dream Societies that linked them together in a special group.

Sweat lodges full of steam were also thought to make a person pure, and were often used before special ceremonies. In the Sun Dance women cut down a forked tree which was then erected within a circle. For days dancers would circle the pole seeking a vision. Some would pierce their chest muscles with skewers which were attached to the pole by leather thongs. They would dance, pulling on the thongs, until they ripped out of their chests. Another dance was the Scalp Dance in which scalps of enemies were paraded and presented to women of the tribe as trophies.

**Q**

**1.** Look at **Sources A** and **C**. Why did Native Americans think a ritual dance was important before a hunt?

**2.** Explain the importance of: *visions*, *medicine* and *dances*.

**3.** In what ways did the environment of the Plains tribes affect their beliefs?

### SOURCE B

▲ *A Blackfeet medicine man or shaman.*

### SOURCE C

There was a time when we could change between being buffalo and Lakota. And then, at one time, the buffalo felt sorry for people because we couldn't make it on our own. So they decided to help us out and offered themselves to us. They said, 'You can use us to maintain your existence. And if you do so in a respectful way it will be all right. But don't ever lose that. If you do, we will go away'.

▲ *Fred Dubray, a modern Lakota, in* Natural Born Americans, *Channel 4 (2000).*

**15**

## 2. AMONGST THE TREES ...

*It is said the animals met to talk about how they were hunted.*

*Each animal decided that if it was not killed with proper respect it would inflict a disease on people. Each animal chose its disease...*

*But Chipmunk said no one hunted him. He had no quarrel with people.*
*This angered the other animals. They scratched Chipmunk's back. That's why all Chipmunks have stripes on their backs.*

### RESPECTFUL HUNTERS

The legend of Chipmunk was important to the Cherokee people. It helped explain why diseases happened. It suggested things to do to stop disease. Many similar stories existed amongst Woodland, and other Native Americans. Some believed bears had once been people. Before they finally changed into bears they taught people special songs to sing. If sung respectfully even bears would allow hunters to kill them for food.

### FORCES OF CREATION AND DEATH

Most Woodland people believed in a Creator who had made the world and a 'life force' that existed in all living things. Plants were thought to bring healing. Animals might bring death if treated disrespectfully. Animals of the night, such as owls, were especially feared as witches.

Some called the Creator, Manito. But the Shawnee thought the Creator was female. **Cannibal** ice giants, the Windigowan, were feared and, among the Algonkian people, there was a great fear of witches.

Groups such as the Iroquois False Face societies believed they knew how to cure sickness. Each spring and autumn the False Faces visited every family to cure illness. Anyone cured was expected to join the society. The masks they wore were often copied from dreams.

**SOURCE D**

▲ *A mask worn by a member of an Iroquois False Face society.*

### THE THREE SISTERS

Woodland tribes were farmers as well as hunters. Amongst the Iroquois, the Three Sisters were worshipped. These were the spirits which were thought to make maize, beans and squash grow.

### 3. SPIRITS OF THE DESERT

For Pueblo farming tribes of the South-West, such as the Zuni and the Hopi, rain brought life to their crops. Special ceremonies in underground rooms, called 'kivas', were believed to make rain return. Dancers, dressed as spirits called 'kachinas', carried out ritual dances believed to bring rain.

Amongst the Hopis, Snake Dancers released snakes into the desert to take the message to the rain spirit that the crops needed water.

### OWLS, HEROES AND DANCERS

In the 1870s Apache scouts working for the American General Crook refused to go any further until a photographer, Frank Randall, had released an owl he had caught and tied to his saddle. To the Apache owls, coyotes, bears and snakes contained the spirits of witches. They believed that only special medicine men, or shamans, knew how to protect them from such dangers.

Most Apache believed in two great spirits: 'Child of the Water' and his mother, 'White Painted Woman'. In Apache beliefs these had defeated monsters that had once lived on the earth. Some groups also believed in a spirit called 'Life Giver' and two god-heroes called 'Changing Woman' and her son, 'Slayer of Monsters'. In many ceremonies these were called on to protect the Apache.

Amongst the Western Apache, masked dancers dressed as mountain spirits called 'gans'. These 'gan dancers' were thought to communicate with the mountain spirits, who would keep disease and evil spirits away.

## SOURCE E

Painted Zuni wooden lightning symbol from a 'kiva'.

## SOURCE F

Pueblo 'kachina' doll given to children to teach them about beliefs of the tribe.

The Pueblo tribes kept captive eagles in cages so they could easily get hold of eagle feathers to use in their rituals.

## Q

**1.** What does the Cherokee story of the Chipmunk tell us about their understanding of the world?

**2.** Why do you think kachina dolls were given to children?

**3.** Explain how the different life experiences and environments led to the beliefs of the Native Americans of:

■ the Woodlands
■ the South-Western deserts and mountains.

# The sacred red tomahawk

**YOUR MISSION: to discover how war was treated as a sacred activity by Plains tribes.**

It was 1876 and the Battle of the Little Bighorn was raging between the Seventh Cavalry and the warriors of the Lakota and Cheyenne. Suddenly a Cheyenne warrior, named Yellow Nose, raced his horse forward and seized one of the US flags. Riding amongst the soldiers he leaned this way and that, touching the soldiers without killing them. Few other warriors that day gained such a name for bravery.

## TYPES OF WAR
- to capture better camp sites and hunting grounds;
- to capture horses;
- to show the bravery of warriors.

Plains tribes rarely took part in large battles. Instead they carried out raids on neighbouring tribes. There were two types of raids: horse raids and scalp raids.

*Horse raids* were common. They did not need a chief's agreement. It involved few warriors.

*Scalp raids* were to seek revenge on an enemy tribe. On such a raid the dead enemy were **scalped** and their scalps brought home. As important was the numbers of 'coups counted'. This was when a warrior touched an enemy with a stick, or hand. It was thought a greater sign of honour than actually killing. It crushed the enemy's spiritual power.

## NEW WORDS

**SCALP:** to cut off the hair and skin on top of the head. It was thought to weaken an enemy's spirit in the afterlife and replace the spirits of tribe members killed by enemies.
**TOMAHAWK:** a fighting axe.

## SOURCE B

About 15 days ago they had a battle with the Omahas. They killed 65 men and took 25 women prisoner. They took the 65 scalps and hung them on small poles, which their women held in their hands when they danced.

⏶ *Joseph Whitehouse, in 1804, describing a Lakota scalp dance.*

## SOURCE A

⏶ *'Scalping', painted by Peter Rindisbacher in the 19th century.*

## PREPARING FOR WAR

For warriors, war was a sacred duty. Dances and sacrifices were made before an attack to try to get help from spirit helpers. Medicine bundles were carried to bring good luck in battle. Faces and bodies were painted to show a warrior's experiences and to ask for protection from spirit helpers. Different feathers were worn to show acts of bravery in the past. War shirts were fringed with the hair of dead enemies.

*Four Bears chief of the* ➤ *Mandan dressed for war. The way he was dressed was full of meanings.*

The Lakota war chief, Crazy Horse, went into battle almost naked. He wore no feathers. He took no scalps. He carried a pebble tied behind his ear. He painted his horse with spots like a shower of hail. This was because he believed he had been told in a vision that if he fought this way no bullet could kill him. When he died he was killed by a soldier's bayonet.

**SOURCE C**

*Eagle feather: scalped an enemy. Eagle a spirit helper.*

*Owl feathers: member of Dog Society. Owl a spirit helper.*

*Split turkey feather: wounded by an arrow. Turkey a spirit helper.*

*Six wooden sticks: number of bullet wounds.*

*Horizontal lines: numbers of coups.*

*Wooden knife: wrestled knife from Cheyenne and killed him.*

*Bundle: sacred medicine, believed to bring good luck.*

*Yellow hand: captured prisoners.*

*Red tomahawk: killed men with it.*

## INVESTIGATION

**You are the investigator!**

Design a guide on 'How Native Americans treated war as a sacred activity'.

■ Explain the meaning of counting coups and scalping.

■ Show how preparation for battle was important and what forms it might take.

■ Show how war linked in with other Native American beliefs.

# The impact of war

**YOUR MISSION: to discover how much war affected the lives of Native Americans on the Plains.**

**NEW WORDS**

**THUNDER AND LIGHTNING:** guns, named from the sound and fire they made.

In 1804 the US explorer, Meriweather Lewis, promised Native Americans that the US government would bring peace to warring tribes. One warrior seemed unhappy about this. 'Without wars,' he said, 'how would we choose our chiefs?'

**SOURCE A**

▲ *Hidatsa warrior, Pehriska-Ruhpa. The special head-dress shows he was a member of the Dog Society.*

**SOURCE B**

▲ *The hat that nearly started a war. Worn by the Fox warrior, Kish-Ke-Kosh, 1837.*

## SORTING MEN FROM THE BOYS

It was through war that warriors became leaders of their people. But it must be remembered that chiefs also had to be wise. A man who was thought to have good 'medicine' and to be able to speak with the spirits believed to guard the tribe could also rise to be a leader. Boys who refused to become warriors could dress and act as women. These were called 'berdaches', or 'a-go-kwa'. They were looked down on by other men. But they were also thought to have 'medicine powers' and to be lucky.

## MAKING MEN 'BELONG'

Warriors joined special clubs or societies such as the Dog Societies of the Hidatsa and Cheyenne. They acted as a police force, supported each other, and gave advice to chiefs who were not warriors.

## MOVING ON

Warfare between tribes caused great movement of Native Americans before any Europeans arrived. In the 18th century, the Lakota were driven West by the Ojibwa. In turn they attacked the Mandan and drove the Cheyenne out onto the Plains. The Blackfeet raided West and drove the Shoshone into the mountains. These conflicts were made worse when Europeans traded guns to one side.

In 1837 there was nearly a war in a US government office in Washington when a group of visiting Lakota noticed that a visiting Fox tribe warrior was wearing a hat taken from a Lakota he had scalped. War was part of life on the Plains.

## SOURCE C

The Shoshone once lived on the buffalo Plains but at the end of the 18th century were driven West into the mountains by the Blackfeet, Atsinas and Hidatsas, who had been given guns by Canadian fur traders.

▲ **D.Duncan, K.Burns, Lewis and Clark, 1997.**

## SOURCE D

A great many snows past, our people were in constant fear. When we hunted buffalo we were often attacked and many of our bravest warriors fell victim to the **'thunder and lightning'** carried by our enemies. Our chief said, 'Let us escape to the mountains. Let us seek their deepest hiding places. There, hidden from our enemies, we can hunt deer.'

▲ *A Shoshone named Faro, in 1804, explains how his tribe escaped from their Native American enemies.*

## INVESTIGATION

**You are the investigator!**

Meriweather Lewis is rather surprised by the warrior's answer in 1804.

Explain to him why the warrior might have said what he did. Mention:

■ How war helps choose leaders.

■ War and men's 'identity'.

■ How European involvement has affected wars between tribes.

■ Wars and movements of tribes.

■ Why successful warriors like war.

**Discussion Point**
In what way has war changed this country over the past 100 years?

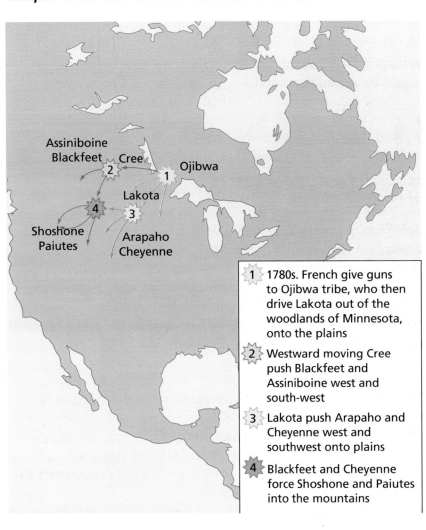

1. 1780s. French give guns to Ojibwa tribe, who then drive Lakota out of the woodlands of Minnesota, onto the plains

2. Westward moving Cree push Blackfeet and Assiniboine west and south-west

3. Lakota push Arapaho and Cheyenne west and southwest onto plains

4. Blackfeet and Cheyenne force Shoshone and Paiutes into the mountains

# 3 MEETINGS AND MURDER

### THIS CHAPTER ASKS

What impact did the first European settlers have on Native Americans?
How did this change between 1500 and 1780?
How were Native Americans affected by new diseases?
How accurate a picture of events do we get from Disney's *Pocahontas*?

### NEW WORDS

**ALLIES:** friends, often military ones.
**PURITANS:** Christians who wanted church services to be simple, and all teaching to come from the Bible.

In November 1620, a party of British people, remembered in US history as the 'Pilgrim Fathers', landed on the east coast of America. They were **Puritans** and had left Britain because they had not been free to worship God as they wished. They faced a hard winter and struggled to survive. Then something amazing happened.

In January 1621, an unknown Native American walked into their camp and welcomed them in English! He had learned the language from other settlers. Two months later the local tribe, the Wampanoag, sent a man named Tisquantum to find out what the newcomers wanted in America. The British called him Squanto and he became a firm friend. He spoke fluent English because he had been kidnapped in 1605 and taken to England. He eventually returned to America where, in 1614, he was kidnapped again by a trader named Hunt. Sold as a slave in Spain, Squanto was rescued by Spanish Christian monks. Through a series of adventures he eventually reached home in 1619 to find that the whole of his tribe, the Patuxet, had died from disease. It was then that Squanto went to live with the Wampanoag.

Through his help the Pilgrim Fathers made an alliance with the Wampanoag, promising to help each other if attacked. Squanto taught the British how to catch local fish and plant corn beside a dead fish to make the seed grow. Squanto soon became quite powerful. He threatened local tribes that, unless they did as he said, he would cause the diseases brought by the British to kill them! The Wampanoag would have killed him but in 1622 Squanto fell ill, while on a trading expedition, and died.

As conflict grew between Europeans and Native Americans in the 17th century, the Europeans carried out many acts of violence. In 1637 the British massacred almost the entire Pequot tribe. In 1641 the Dutch offered money for every Native American scalp brought in. Other payments were made for skinned Native Americans – 'redskins'.

### WHAT THE STORY TELLS US

- The first Europeans often relied on local people for trade, food, advice.
- Others treated Native people badly.
- European diseases killed many Native people.
- Europeans and Native Americans sometimes acted as **allies** in local wars.

## CHANGING RELATIONSHIPS

After Columbus landed in 1492, many Europeans explored North America. They had different plans for this New World.

The Spanish wanted gold and new land. They used Native Americans as slaves. Spanish missionaries aimed to convert Native People into Catholics. The French and Russians were after furs and were more interested in trading than in taking land. The Dutch first traded for fur. But as this ran out, by the 1630s, they took land. The British settlers also wanted land. This soon caused conflict with Native Americans.

In 1622 and 1644 there were wars as the Powhatan people of Virginia (the tribe of Pocahontas) tried to drive out the British.

During the 18th century, as the British and French fought for control of North America, they both used Native Peoples as allies.

**Q**

**1.** Using the text and map, make a timeline showing the development of European influence in North America, 1500–1780.

**2.** Imagine you are Squanto. Retell the story of your relationship with Europeans. Mention both the good and bad things caused to your life by them.

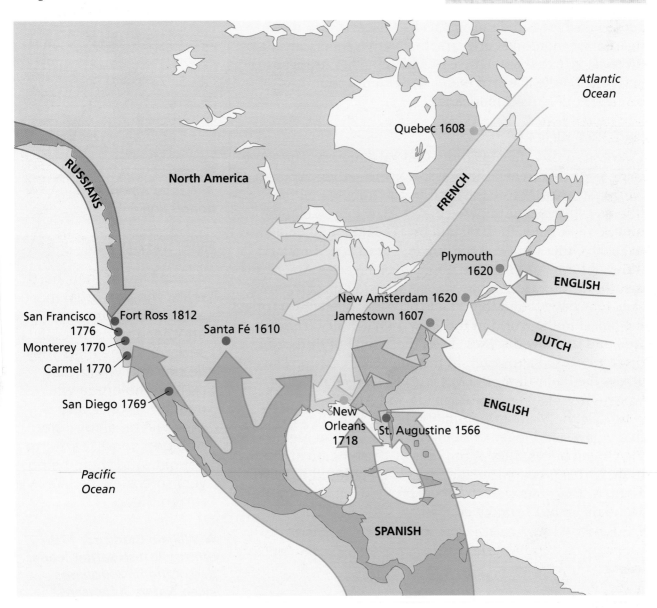

23

# Invisible killers

## DEATH OF A CHIEF

In 1832 the American artist George Catlin stayed with the Mandan people who lived on the edge of the Great Plains. He painted many of them and liked them; finding that they did not lie, steal or cheat. He was especially impressed by a chief named Four Bears. But five years later Four Bears watched every one of his family die … all his wives … all his little children. Broken hearted he starved himself to death. Who had slaughtered Four Bears' warm and welcoming people? Not an army. Not a gun. But a disease. Smallpox had destroyed the Mandan.

## DEATH OF A PEOPLE

Between 1492 and 1900 the Native American population fell by about 95%. Much of this was due to disease. This was because Europeans brought diseases that had never been known before in America. These diseases killed Europeans, but they killed many more Native Americans. This was because, whereas the Europeans had experienced these disease for thousands of years, the Native Americans had no resistance to them. Diseases which made Europeans ill and killed quite a few of them, slaughtered countless numbers of Native Americans.

## INVISIBLE KILLERS

Diseases spread after 1492 into Central America. The same thing happened when the first European settlers reached North America. Before the first French traders met the Illinois tribes they numbered about 20,000. By 1700 their number had fallen to 6,000 and by 1768 it had fallen again to 2,200. Other trappers, trading for furs, carried malaria into California in 1833, and about 20,000 Native Americans died of the disease. Archaeologists working on comparing skeletons have found that Plains tribespeople were amongst the tallest in the world in the early 19th century. They ate well and had few diseases. Then the arrival of European diseases caused a disaster. In the late 1830s smallpox swept across the Plains from the Missouri River to the Pacific North-West. It spread into Canada and Alaska.

In 1804 the Mandan population was 4,500. They lived in five villages and together made up a population bigger than the United States cities of St Louis or Washington at the time. By 1833 their population had been reduced to 2,000. Then, in 1837, European trappers brought smallpox to the Mandan. Only 137 survived.

## NEW WORDS

**GORE:** bloody.
**PERNICIOUS:** wicked.
**POX:** boils and sores.
**TITLE:** right to own something.

## SOURCE A

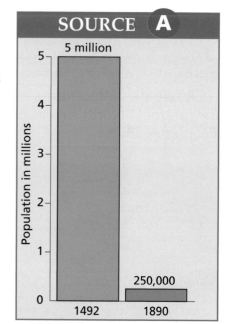

▲ *Native American population.*

## SOURCE B

As they lie on their hard mats, the **pox** breaking and running one into another, their skin sticking to the mats they lie on. And when they turn a whole side will peel off at once and they will be all of a **gore** of blood, most fearful to behold. And then, being very sore they die like rotten sheep.

▲ *William Bradford, 17th-century British settler leader, describing how diseases killed Native Americans.*

## SOURCE C

In sweeping away great multitudes of the natives God has cleared our **title** to this place.

▲ *John Winthrop, 17th-century settler leader.*

## WHAT ABOUT NORTH AMERICAN DISEASES?

Did any diseases go the other way? For a long time it was believed that the sexually transmitted disease, syphilis was a North American disease which spread to Europeans. Now historians and archaeologists are not so sure. In the late 1990s archaeologists digging up a Medieval monastery in Hull found the bones of people who had suffered from syphilis. This was before Columbus discovered America.

## SOURCE D

The woods are almost cleared of these **pernicious** creatures, to make room for a better growth.

▲ *A 17th-century Puritan writer.*

## SOURCE E

Smallpox and measles swept through the Indian nations and killed vast numbers of people within weeks. Often, before tribes had recovered, disease hit them again. This caused an imbalance between tribes and broke the natural relationship they had with the environment. When the White frontier then pushed tribes to the west, they hit back with an aggressiveness and hatred that was alien to their culture.

▲ *N. Bancroft-Hunt, The Indians of the Great Plains, 1981.*

## SOURCE F

*Results of disease*

*Native Americans weakened. Could not fight back.*

*Some Native Americans believed God on side of Europeans.*

*Europeans believed God wanted to remove Native Americans.*

*Large areas deserted for Europeans to settle in.*

*Black slaves brought to America to replace dead Native Americans.*

Many diseases travel from animals to people. Native Americans kept few domesticated animals and so had caught fewer of their diseases.

**Q**

**1.** Read **Sources C** and **D**. How did some Europeans explain why diseases killed many Native people?

**2.** Read **Source E**. According to this historian, how did these experiences change Native people?

**3.** Historians often use the terms 'cause' and 'consequence' to describe why events happen and what they lead to.

  **a.** Explain what 'caused' these diseases to kill Native Americans more than Europeans.

  **b.** Explain what 'consequences' these diseases had for Native Americans and then for European settlers.

# Colours of the wind

**YOUR MISSION: to investigate the accuracy of Disney's film, Pocahontas.**

One of the most famous meetings between a Native American and an English explorer was between a young girl named Matoaka and John Smith in 1607. It took place on the east coast of what the English called 'Virginia'. Matoaka is better known by the pet-name her father used for her. This pet-name means 'little mischief' and in her own language was 'Pocahontas'. In 1995 her story was made into a Disney cartoon. Disney mostly followed the traditional story of Pocahontas and Smith to make a popular cartoon. But how accurate was the traditional story?

## FACT FILE 1

*In 1607 Pocahontas was 11 years old. John Smith was in his forties. He was short, with a beard.*

## FACT FILE 2

*The colonists at Jamestown made no attempt to rescue Smith when he was captured.*

## FACT FILE 3

*Native Americans on the east coast grew corn and fished.*

The descendants of Pocahontas and John Rolfe were called the 'Red Rolfes' by settlers in Virginia. Today there are many descendants of Pocahontas.

**A** *In Pocahontas' village the people grow corn and catch fish.*

John Ratcliffe

**B** *Ratcliff, governor of the Jamestown colony, wants to destroy the Native Americans.*

**C** *Pocahontas falls in love with young John Smith.*

**D** *Pocahontas tells Smith how her people respect nature.*

Kocoum

**E** *Pocahontas is promised in marriage, by her father Powhatan, to a warrior named Kocoum.*

**F** *Pocahontas saves John Smith from being executed by her father. She stops a war with the English who have come to rescue Smith.*

## FACT FILE 4

*Ratcliff wanted peace with Native Americans. Smith was more violent.*

## FACT FILE 5

*Smith made no mention at the time of Pocahontas saving him. He only said it 17 years later. Then he made it one of three times his life was saved by beautiful women.*

## FACT FILE 6

*In 1612 Pocahontas was kidnapped by the English. She met and married a man named John Rolfe in 1614. She became a Christian and changed her name to Rebecca.*

## FACT FILE 7

*Pocahontas travelled to England. She died of fever at Gravesend, Kent, in March, 1617.*

## FACT FILE 8

*While Pocahontas was in England an enemy said she was really married to a warrior – Kocoum.*

## FACT FILE 9

*Powhatan was not the name of a chief but of a group of tribes.*

## INVESTIGATION

**You are the investigator!**

How accurate is the traditional story of Pocahontas and Smith in the film?

■ What parts do you think were true?

■ What parts not true?

■ Overall, how accurate do you think it is?

# WHEN WORLDS COLLIDE

**THIS CHAPTER ASKS**

How did relations between Europeans and Native Americans change between 1780 and 1900?
How and why was Native American culture destroyed?

## NEW WORDS

**MASSACRE:** to murder people in a savage way.
**RESERVATIONS:** small areas of often poor-quality land on which tribes were forced to live.

*Shawnee chief, Tecumseh tries to unite tribes to protect their land. Killed in battle in 1812.*

*1834: USA forces all East coast tribes to move West. Thousands die on the 'Trail of Tears'.*

*Seminole tribe fights USA in Florida, 1817–58. US forced to withdraw.*

*1848: California Gold Rush. Miners destroy local Native Americans.*

*After 1851 tribes forced onto reservations. Land that had been promised to them forever is taken away.*

*1864: Colorado Volunteers massacre helpless Cheyennes at Sand Creek.*

*War on Northern Plains. Lakota Chief, Red Cloud forces USA to sign Fort Laramie Treaty, 1868, and withdraw.*

*1874: Gold found in Black Hills; sacred area promised to Lakota. USA attacks all tribes refusing to leave Black Hills.*

*1876: Lakota and Cheyenne win Battle of Little Bighorn. But are later defeated.*

*1877: Nez Perce War in North-West. Tribe fails in plan to escape to Canada.*

*1876–86: Apache War led by Geronimo. Defeated and imprisoned.*

*Ghost Dancers believe Europeans will be driven away. Massacred at Wounded Knee in 1890.*

*How America was taken from Native Americans, 1780–1890.*

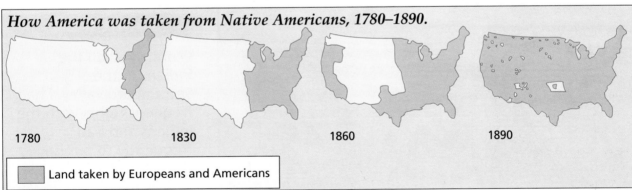

| 1780 | 1830 | 1860 | 1890 |

Land taken by Europeans and Americans

**Q** **1.** Look carefully at the maps. Explain how much the situation of Native Americans changed between 1780 and 1890.

**2.** Describe the ways in which the freedom of Native Americans was destroyed in this period of time. Mention:

■ Wars fought.

■ Promises to tribes broken.

■ Native American resistance.

■ Native American defeats.

A peace treaty between the USA and the Seminoles was not signed until 1934, making it the longest war in modern history.

**29**

# Traders, or invaders?

## CONFLICT IN CALIFORNIA

Until 1846 California was a part of Mexico. Then it became part of the USA. Before this happened though, in 1839, a Swiss immigrant called John Sutter set up a trading post in North-Eastern California, near the Sacramento River at a place he called 'New Helvetia', but which soon came to be called Sutter's Fort.

The Mexicans were happy to let him do this. Ever since the late 18th century, the Spanish and then the Mexicans (who had gained independence from Spain) had been trying to conquer and control the Native Americans in what we now call California. All along the coast the Spanish had set up missions from which the local tribes could be ruled. For the Spanish this had meant making them Christians and forcing them to live like Europeans. Near each Mission was a Presidio, a fort from which soldiers could control the local people. The Mexicans were happy to let Sutter set up his fort and they hoped he would help keep the local tribes from attacking Mexican settlements.

## SOURCE A

▲ *A modern reconstruction of Sutter's Fort. Inside were blacksmiths' and carpenters' shops, a bakery, distillery and a blanket-making factory.*

## SUTTER – A NEW 'CHIEF'?

Sutter soon employed hundreds of Native Americans. Some were 'vaqueros' (cowboys), some worked in his fields, others were trappers, fishermen, weavers and cooks. He paid them with food, and clothes, and gave them homes. One group were given weapons and uniforms and acted as soldiers. Sutter used them to punish local tribes who disobeyed him.

## NEW WORDS

**BECK:** command or order.
**DISTILLERY:** place where alcohol is made.
**INTIMIDATED:** frightened.

## SOURCE B

He has at his **beck** four or five Indian tribes, whom he has won by kindness and also **intimidated** by punishments.

▲ *A report by a traveller who visited Sutter's Fort in 1841.*

## SOURCE C

I controlled all the Indians in the Sacramento valley. I had frequent fights with the Indians and had frequently to punish them for stealing cattle. At this time I had power of life and death over both Indians and White people. The Spanish [Mexicans] were very much surprised when they saw my Indian soldiers, especially because one of them could read and write, which many could not do.

▲ *John Sutter looking back in 1876.*

Sutter acted like a new 'chief' with his own 'tribe' of followers. He made friends with some local Native American tribes. He fought with others. He supported some tribes in their quarrels with their enemies. He made no attempt to convert the tribes to Christianity as the Spanish had done, or to greatly change their lifestyles. They were his allies, or enemies, depending on how they fitted in with his plans. By 1847, Sutter employed about 50 European settlers and had control over perhaps 20,000 local Native Americans. Of these about 500 were directly employed by him.

## SUTTER – CHANGING LIVES?

Sutter was happy to use the local tribes, not to change them. But changes happened anyway. His fort soon became a busy centre. He set up a blanket-making factory. Native Americans employed by Sutter were beginning to work and act like Europeans. His Native American soldiers wore uniforms, marched and paraded.

The local tribes began to rely on his new goods. Those who obeyed Sutter were given some. Sutter made allies of the Ochecames tribe around his fort and used them to attack and enslave other Native Americans.

Even before the Gold Rush of 1849, settlers arriving at his fort began to take land from the local tribes. These new farms, or 'ranchos', also used local people as workers, but after 1848 the settlers began to drive Native people off the land. Although Sutter had respected the rights of Native Americans to own land, the new settlers did not. When gold was discovered at one of Sutter's mills, in January 1848, these changes were to turn into an avalanche.

When Sutter left Switzerland in 1834 he remembered to bring all his clothes and books to America – but not his wife and five children!

## SOURCE D

I had about 4,000 sheep. From the wool we made our own blankets. After great difficulty I established a factory. I taught the natives how to weave.

▲ *John Sutter. The blankets were traded for furs with local tribes.*

**Q** **1.** Look at **Sources B** and **C**. 'Sutter's impact on Native Americans was a mix of positive and negative.' Show how this might be thought from this evidence. Which source would you find most reliable for assessing his impact?

**2.** How great an impact did Sutter have on Native people? *Think about:* differences between him and the Spanish; his use of power; new goods and skills; new settlers.

### Discussion Point
How does Western trade with less developed countries affect the people who live there today?

- Spanish missions from which Native Americans were controlled
- ◪ Sutter's Fort
- Modern boundary of California

*Sacramento River*

# Gold and blood

**YOUR MISSION: to discover how the lives of Native Americans in California were changed by the discovery of gold in 1848.**

## NEW WORDS

**GAME:** wild animals hunted, e.g. deer.
**PANNED:** searched for gold in rivers.
**SQUAWS:** word used for Native American women.

Historians sometimes talk about 'accelerators' in History. These are events which speed up a process and cause great changes to happen quickly. In California this accelerator started on 24 January, 1848, at a water-powered saw mill being built on the American River, a day's ride to the east of Sutter's Fort. It was the discovery of gold.

Until this event the Spanish, the Mexicans and John Sutter himself had had an impact on the lives of Native Americans in California, but what now happened was to have a far greater one. Once the news of gold leaked out, tens of thousands of outsiders poured into California. At first Native Americans **panned** for gold too. But the newcomers stole their land, murdered Native tribes and destroyed their world. And it all happened in about ten years.

## SOURCE B

The Whites began to gather up the Indians. They drove them like cattle. They shot the old people who could not make the trip. They would shoot children who were getting tired. They killed all who tried to get away.

▲ *Native American tradition of how tribes were driven from land wanted by miners and ranchers.*

## SOURCE C

Whites stole food, they took the **game**, and worst of all they stole the young girls. This created bad feelings towards the Whites and there were killings. The land was good and White families wanted to build homes and start farms. The Indians were in the way.

▲ *Eveline Mota of the Maidu people remembers stories told her by her great grandmother.*

## SOURCE D

The Indians had to move around to hunt and gather food. Later on, White people kept moving into more and more of the places and we couldn't camp around those places anymore. When the Indians were told to leave a place they just headed farther into the mountains. Soon they told us to move again.

▲ *Traditions of the Kumeyaay people.*

## SOURCE A

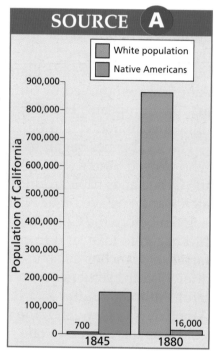

White population
Native Americans

Population of California

900,000
800,000
700,000
600,000
500,000
400,000
300,000
200,000
100,000
0

700       16,000
1845       1880

▲ *The population of California in 1845 and 1880.*

## SOURCE E

The Indians never hurt anything but the White people destroy all. They blast rocks and scatter them on the earth. They make roads. They dig as much as they wish. They don't care how much the ground cries out.

▲ *Experiences of the Wintu people.*

## SOURCE F

A band of Mountain Indians made a raid on some of the miners and robbed them of a horse and other valuables, killing one miner and wounding another. The miners followed the Indians into the mountains. Then they found their settlement and killed old men, **squaws** and children.

▲ *A miner's account of a massacre of Native Americans near Big Oak Flat, in 1850.*

## SOURCE G

The California valley did not have a single Indian war. It can boast however a hundred or two of as brutal butchering on the part of our honest miners and brave pioneers as any other area. When now and then one of them [Native Americans] plucked up courage to defend his wife and little ones, sufficient excuse was offered for the miners and settlers to band and shoot down any Indian they met, old or young, innocent or guilty, friendly or hostile.

▲ *Written by the US historian, H.H. Bancroft, in the 1880s.*

## SOURCE H

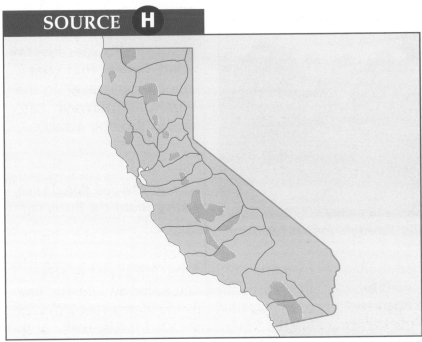

▲ *Outlined areas show land given up by Native Americans in treaties with the US government, 1851. The dark areas show areas left to the tribes. But the US government refused to agree the treaties and secretly locked them away. Settlers went on stealing land from the Native peoples.*

The US army burned the homes of Native Americans in the Yosemite Valley as recently as 1906. And the last Shoshone raids on White farms took place in 1915.

## INVESTIGATION

**You are the investigator!**

You have been commissioned to design a memorial to the ways in which the discovery of gold changed the lives of Native Americans in California. Show:

- The discovery of gold.
- Outsiders flooding in.
- Native people forced off their land.
- Resistance leading to massacres.
- Hunting ruined as animals driven away.
- Damage to the environment.
- The kinds of people responsible.

The memorial could be either:

- a banner with different panels
- a stained glass window
- a series of statues
- A group of poems.

Use all the evidence to help you.

# Wars to save the buffalo

It was 1866 and the Lakota chief, Red Cloud, was angry. He asked his medicine man how many soldiers he and his warriors could kill. The medicine man returned from time spent alone and said, 'I have ten dead soldiers, five in each hand'. He offered his empty hands to Red Cloud. The chief was angry. 'Ten are too few to share between so many of my warriors'. He sent the medicine man away three times until, at last, he returned saying, 'I have a hundred dead soldiers in my hands'. Red Cloud said it was enough.

## RED CLOUD'S WAR

Why was Red Cloud so angry? Soldiers of the USA were building forts along roads across the northern Plains; the new railways were beginning to spread across land that belonged to Native Americans such as the Lakota, Cheyenne and Arapaho. The new roads and railways disturbed the animals that Native Americans hunted. More than this, Red Cloud feared that the settlers moving across his lands would soon begin to take land. This had always been how Native Americans had been treated. Red Cloud was determined to stop this.

## SOURCE B

The white men have crowded the Indians back. Now our last hunting ground is to be taken from us. Our women and children will starve, but I prefer to die fighting rather than by starvation.

▲ *Red Cloud, to US officials at Fort Laramie, 1866.*

## SOURCE A

▲ *An attack on a wagon travelling through 'Indian Territory', drawn in the 19th century.*

## SOURCE C

The cause of our troubles is the Powder River road. If the Great Father [US president] stops the Powder River road, I know that your people can travel on the iron road [railway] without being attacked.

▲ *Chief Pawnee Killer, 1867, talking about the Bozeman Trail.*

In particular Red Cloud objected to the Bozeman Trail. This was a road, built in 1863–65, which led to the newly opened gold mines in Montana. In 1866 the US army built three forts along this road, which ran through the Native American hunting grounds of the Powder River country.

Between 1866–68 Red Cloud led hundreds of warriors in attacks on travellers along this road and on the forts. In December 1866 they **ambushed** and killed 80 soldiers. The soldiers called this the 'Fetterman Massacre', Native Americans called it 'The battle of the hundred in the hands' after the medicine man's promise. In 1867 the US army fought off attacks on haycutters from Fort C.F. Smith and woodcutters from Fort Phil Kearny.

## SOURCE D

▲ *Native Americans attacking a train on the Southern Pacific Railway, Arizona. Published in a French magazine in 1906.*

## SOURCE E

The white man is coming out here so fast that nothing can stop him. Those in the West need to communicate with those in the East. That is why they build these roads, railroads and telegraphs.

▲ *US General Hancock, 1866*

Red Cloud's War shut the Bozeman Trail. In 1868 the US government agreed the Fort Laramie Treaty. This closed the trail and the three forts along it. It set up the 'Great Sioux Reservation' which would remain a Native American area for ever. This included the Black Hills regarded as sacred by the tribes. Red Cloud had won.

### THE SPREAD OF THE RAILWAYS

In the 1860s, railways began to be built across both the Northern and Southern Plains. They frightened the buffalo and carried settlers into Native American land. In the north the Union Pacific Railroad was laid across Nebraska in 1867. The Southern Pacific Railway crossed the lands of the Kiowas, Comanches and Southern Cheyenne.

One Cheyenne warrior attempted to rope one of the 'Iron Horses' and pull it from its tracks. Instead, he was pulled from his pony and dragged along until he managed to free himself. Others discovered that if the iron tracks were pulled up the train would crash. In 1867, warriors caused a train to crash and killed everyone inside, except two men who managed to escape. But the railways continued to be built and defended by the US army.

**Q**

**1.** Look at **Sources C** and **E**. Why do you think Pawnee Killer feared the road more than the railway? How do Hancock's words suggest the rail was a threat too?

**2.** Use the sources and the text to write a speech that Red Cloud might have made at Fort Laramie in 1868.

■ Explain why he opposes the road, the railway, the new forts.

■ Say what he has done to stop them.

■ Say what he demands from the government in return for peace.

## WHY WERE THE BUFFALO DESTROYED?

In 1887 New York's Museum of Natural History sent a hunting party to get a buffalo skin for its collection. After three months hunting they gave up. They could not find a single buffalo. In 1800 there had been 60 million buffalo. In 1889 there were only 835 left alive in the USA. How was this possible?

European settlers had once encouraged Native Americans to trap beavers for the making of fashionable hats. But beavers had been made almost **extinct**. So fur traders turned to the buffalo. As cow-hide was more valuable than bull-hide, hunters killed many more female buffalo, which disrupted buffalo breeding.

During the American Civil War, hunters were paid to kill buffalo to feed soldiers in the Western forts. After the war ended, in 1865, the same hunters killed them to feed railroad workers. The most famous hunter, William 'Buffalo Bill' Cody killed 4,280 in only 17 months.

The growth of railways, after 1865, disrupted the herds and brought holiday makers on buffalo killing trips. Thomas Nixon, of Kansas, killed 120 in 40 minutes. Between 1872 and 1874 over 3 million buffalo hides were collected. In 1850 it had been 100,000 hides. The US army and government encouraged the slaughter. They knew it would destroy the lives of the Plains tribes. To survive, they would be forced to live like Europeans. Their old way of life would be gone forever.

The buffalo herds on the Southern Plains were destroyed by 1875; the Northern ones by 1885. The last wild herd was slaughtered in 1897 in Lost Park, Colorado. The only ones left were those few protected in National Parks and by some landowners.

### NEW WORDS

**COYOTE:** animal like a small wolf.
**EXTINCT:** all killed.

### SOURCE F

▲ *A vast pile of buffalo skulls.*

### SOURCE G

Your young men have killed my animals, the elk, the deer, the antelope, my buffalo. They do not kill them to eat them; they leave them to rot where they fall.

▲ *The Crow chief, Bear Tooth, 1867.*

### SOURCE H

It would be a great step forward in the civilisation of the Indians and the preservation of peace if there was not a single buffalo in existence.

▲ *US politician, James Throckmorton, 1876.*

### SOURCE I

▲ *Hunting buffalo from a train.*

THINKING IT THROUGH

## THE WAR TO SAVE THE BUFFALO

On the Southern Plains, the Southern Cheyenne, Arapaho, Kiowas and Comanches attacked farms, ranches and hunters between 1865 and 1875. They sought revenge for the bloody massacre of over 100 Cheyenne and Arapaho women and children at Sand Creek, in 1864, by Colonel Chivington and his Colorado Volunteers. They also tried to protect their buffalo herds from destruction

## THE RED RIVER WAR, 1874–75

Kiowa chiefs Satank, Big Tree, Satanta and Lone Wolf led warriors off their reservation in Oklahoma and Kansas to hunt buffalo in Texas and to attack buffalo hunters and settlers. Later in the Red River War (1874), 700 warriors attacked buffalo hunters at a fort called Adobe Walls but were beaten. The hunters' rifles were so powerful that one bullet knocked a warrior off his horse a mile from the fort. The US army paid Native American Tonkawa scouts to find the Kiowa's camp at Palo Duro Canyon. There they destroyed their tipis and slaughtered a thousand horses. The war was over.

The defeated tribes surrendered at Fort Sill. Their property was burned. Their horses were shot. Chiefs were locked in an open roofed building and fed on chunks of raw meat. Many were imprisoned. Within ten years the great leaders of the Kiowas and Comanches had been defeated, the buffalo were gone, the Plains tribes' way of life, destroyed.

## AND WHAT NEXT?

But the Southern Plains tribes were not the only ones in trouble. At the Fort Laramie meeting in 1868 one North Plains chief had suggested that White people would really like to put Native Americans on wheels so they could be moved out of the way whenever it was thought necessary. Now gold had been discovered in the Black Hills of Dakota. The Lakota had been offered $6 million to sell the hills, although one mine alone was actually worth $500 million a year. But the Black Hills were not for sale. The war to save the buffalo had failed. Would the war to save the Black Hills succeed?

By 1877, Southern Cheyenne buffalo hunters were forced to catch and eat **coyotes** because they could no longer find any buffalo.

**SOURCE J**

▲ *Body of a scalped buffalo hunter, found near Fort Dodge, Kansas.*

**Q**

**1.** What does **Source H** mean? How **(a)** useful, **(b)** reliable is this evidence to a historian?

**2.** Draw a spidergram to show the causes of the destruction of the buffalo. Underneath it explain the consequences of this for Plains tribes?

# What happened at the Little Bighorn?

**YOUR MISSION: to find out what the Battle of the Little Bighorn was really like**

## NEW WORDS

**COMMAND:** group of soldiers.
**SACRED:** holy.

On Sunday, 25 June, 1876 the Lakota and their Cheyenne allies killed Lieutenant Colonel Custer and his entire **command** of 260 men of the Seventh Cavalry.

Gold had been discovered in the Black Hills in 1874. These lands were **sacred** to the Lakota, and the Fort Laramie Treaty (1868) had promised them to Native Americans. White miners poured in. The US government sent in soldiers to protect the miners from the attacks of angry Lakota. It was decided that any Native American who refused to move to a reservation would be treated as a 'hostile', at war with the USA.

Three Army groups moved against the Lakota and their allies. On 17 June, one group, led by General Crook, were defeated at the Battle of the Rosebud river. Another group (the Seventh Cavalry under Custer) was ordered to ride ahead and find the 'hostiles' – *but not to attack*.

Custer's long, golden hair earned him the name, 'Yellow Hair', but he had cut his hair before the battle in which he died.

## SOURCE **A**

▲ *An artist's impression of the battle. It shows the soldiers grouped around Custer in a 'last stand'. But was it really like this?*

Custer ignored his orders. When he reached a huge 'hostile' village he divided his soldiers. He sent 115 troopers, under Captain Benteen, to search for more 'hostiles'. Another 140, under Major Reno, were ordered to attack the eastern end of the village. These were soon beaten back. Custer, with the rest, rode round the village intending to attack from its other end. He never made it. Within one hour Custer and all his men were dead. The only survivor was a horse named Comanche. Reno and Benteen were surrounded, but rescued two days later.

How can we find out about the battle? From Indian accounts and drawings done by warriors who were there? From evidence found by archaeologists in 1983? What was the battle really like?

## SOURCE B

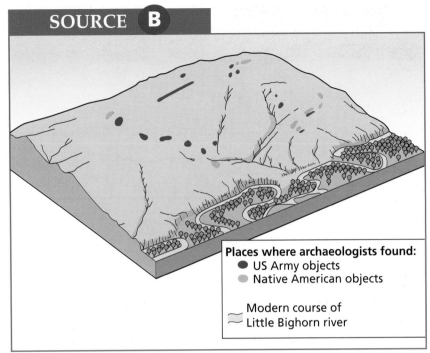

**Places where archaeologists found:**
- ● US Army objects
- ● Native American objects

〰 Modern course of Little Bighorn river

▲ *Places where archaeologists found evidence in 1983.*

## SOURCE C

▼*Map drawn by a Native American warrior present at the battle.*

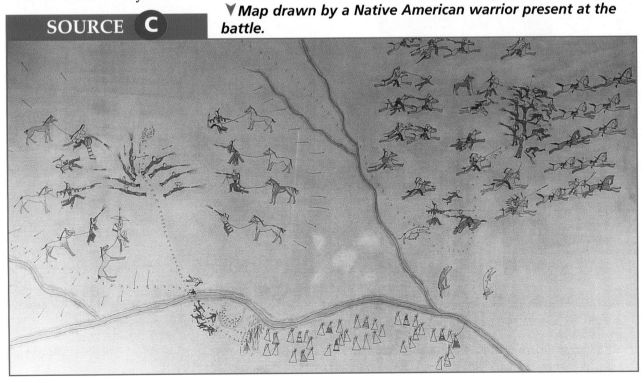

## SOURCE **D**

◄ *Drawn by a Native American present at the battle.*

## SOURCE **F**

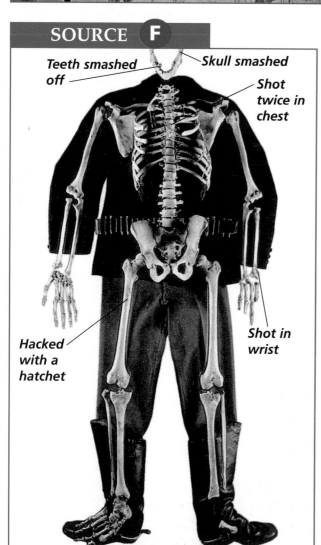

**Teeth smashed off**

**Skull smashed**

**Shot twice in chest**

**Hacked with a hatchet**

**Shot in wrist**

▲ *A skeleton of a Cavalry soldier discovered in 1983. The right thigh bone (right) shows marks made by a hatchet.*

## SOURCE **E**

▲ *Drawn by a Native American present at the battle, showing dead soldiers.*

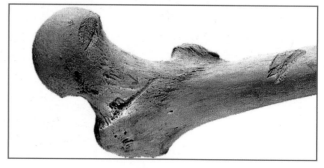

## SOURCE **G**

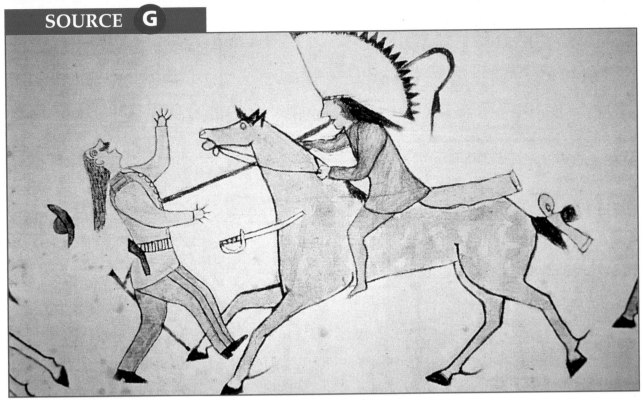

▲ *Drawn by a Native American present at the battle.*

## SOURCE **H**

We were as many as the leaves on the trees.

▲ *Native American, Crow King. There were about 2,000 warriors.*

## SOURCE **I**

After driving some soldiers across the river we charged the different soldiers and drove them in confusion. These became foolish. Many threw away their guns and raised their hands saying, 'Sioux, pity us; take us prisoner'. We killed them all.

▲ *Lakota warrior, Red Horse.*

Custer had a reputation for hard fighting and spending hours in the saddle. His soldiers called him 'Iron Butt' !

## **I**NVESTIGATION

**You are the investigator!**

Use all the evidence to discover what the battle was like.

■ How did the cavalry attack?

■ How well was the village defended?

■ How did Custer's men die – in a last stand together, or scattered and trying to escape?

■ How were the dead treated by the Lakota and Cheyenne?

**41**

# 5 DEATH OF A PEOPLE?

## THIS CHAPTER ASKS

How was the Native American way of life destroyed after 1880?

What is life like as a modern Native American?

The Battle of the Little Bighorn (1876) changed nothing. Within a year the Lakota were defeated. Earlier, in 1873, the Modocs of Northern California were crushed after a short, but bloody, war. In 1877, the Nez Perce of Idaho were driven to war – despite the attempts of their chief, Joseph, to keep the peace – and were defeated.

In 1878, the Bannocks and Paiutes of Idaho and Oregon were defeated. In 1879, other Bannocks and Shoshone, in Idaho, were crushed. In 1886, the last Apache chief, Geronimo surrendered after wars in Arizona and New Mexico. The 'Indian Wars' were over. What now followed was the destruction of what remained of the Native American way of life.

1. 1883 Sun Dance banned on reservations.

2. after 1885 tribes on reservations forced to farm not hunt.

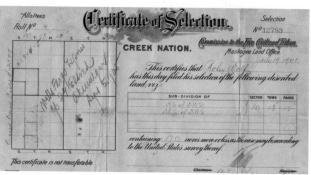

3. 1887. Reservations divided amongst individual Native people to destroy tribal way of life.

4. 1880s. Indian children forced into boarding schools. Made to live, dress and talk like 'White people'.

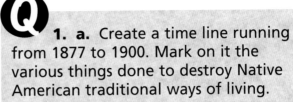

**Q** **1. a.** Create a time line running from 1877 to 1900. Mark on it the various things done to destroy Native American traditional ways of living.

**b.** Choose the three you think would have been most destructive and explain why.

6. 1890 Lakota Ghost Dancers massacred by the US army at Wounded Knee Creek.

5. 1888 Paiute holy man Wovoka claimed if tribes would dance and sing certain songs the Whites would vanish and buffalo and dead relatives would return. This 'Ghost Dance' idea spread.

7. 1897 Paiute Chief, Tom Chocktoot, gaoled for carrying out traditional Native healing ceremonies.

# Native Americans today

In 1492, when Columbus reached the Americas, the number of Native Americans in North America was at least five million. By 1890 it had collapsed to 250,000. In the same time the number of foreign settlers and their descendants had risen to 75 million. It looked as if Native Americans would soon vanish.

But they did not vanish. What is it like to be a Native American today? The question, of course, is too complicated to answer properly, but here are some aspects of Native American life today to get you *started* on answering this question.

## NEW WORDS

**CASINO:** a place to gamble in.
**CULTURE:** way of life.
**SQUALOR:** dirt, disease.

## SOURCE B

In the 1970s new legal help groups, such as the Native American Rights Fund, won cases before the (US) Indians Claims Commission. It now settled land claims arising from broken treaties – the Lakota received $105 million and tribes in Maine were awarded $40 million.

▲ *D. Murdoch,* **North American Indians,** *1995.*

## SOURCE A

If the readers of this book should ever chance to see the poverty, the hopelessness and the **squalor** of a modern Indian reservation, they may find it possible to understand the reasons why [this has happened].

▲ *Dee Brown in the introduction to his book,* Bury My Heart at Wounded Knee, *1970. In this famous book he told the history of how Native Americans had been badly treated and robbed of their land.*

## SOURCE C

▲ *Modern Native American dancer at a powwow. These meetings celebrate Native American culture and traditions. During the 1990s they were attended by 90% of Native Americans.*

## SOURCE D

▲ *Modern Native American casino. US gambling law does not apply to reservations, and one third of reservations have organised gambling. The New England Mashuntucket Pequots earn $600 million a month from slot machines alone.*

## SOURCE E

▲ Modern painting entitled 'The World is in your Hands'. Many people have become interested in Native American beliefs about the environment.

## SOURCE G

In 1989, the average household income for Indians was $19,897 compared with $30,056 for the rest of the US population. During the same year 31.6% of American Indians lived below the poverty line, compared with 13.1% for the rest of the US population.

▲ The Orange County Register [a Californian newspaper], 25 August, 2000.

In August 2000, the brain of Ishi, last of the Californian Yahi tribe, which had been kept in a museum since his death in 1916 was returned for Native American burial.

## SOURCE F

5 times more likely to have heart disease.

3 times more likely to die as a baby.

5 times more likely to have alcohol problems.

8 times more likely to have liver disease.

▲ Native Americans face more poverty and health problems than the Average US citizen.

**Q**

**1.** Look at **Source A**. What evidence supports Dee Brown's opinion about the problems facing modern Native Americans?

**2.** From what you know about the history of the treatment of Native Americans, explain possible reasons why they might face such problems today.

**3.** What evidence is there for changes for the better for Native Americans since Dee Brown wrote his book?

**4.** In your own words, explain how much the lives of Native Americans have been changed in the past 500 years. Mention:
- population
- control of land
- ways of life
- beliefs
- life today.

# Index

INDEX